The L(
Instruction book

The Lovers' Little Instruction Book

Cindy Francis

HarperCollins*Publishers*

HarperCollins*Publishers*
77–85 Fulham Palace Road,
Hammersmith, London W6 8JB

First published in the UK by Thorsons 1994
This edition 2000

1 3 5 7 9 10 8 6 4 2

© Cindy Francis 1993

Cindy Francis asserts the moral right to be
identified as the author of this work

A catalogue record for this book
is available from the British Library

ISBN 0 00 710094 9

Printed and bound in Great Britain by
Martins the Printers Ltd, Berwick upon Tweed

For Aunt Sarah and Uncle Irwin
who, after 44 years of marriage,
still treat each other like newlyweds

Introduction

It has always interested me that the happy and unhappy couples I know both have, generally speaking, the same problems. The happy couples aren't richer or better looking or smarter. They just do things differently. And they've learned some lessons that have helped them to have a better life together.

This little book is designed to teach you what they do and what they've learned.

Since the publication of my previous books, many of you have asked me to write a book specifically for couples. I've been greatly helped in this by a 'success journal' I've kept for some time in which I've written what I've learned from my own marriage and from life.

I have also been helped by a number of happily married friends and relatives and by numerous marriage counsellors who were kind enough to share their thoughts. In addition, I have read lots of books and journals to learn the valuable lessons they have to teach.

Here, then, are my instructions for lovers. I hope you'll enjoy them, and more importantly, I hope you'll put them to use in your own relationship. I wish you lots of joy and lots of love.

Show your love by *listening*.

Don't wait until Friday night to be loving – be loving *all* the time!

Accept each other as you are.

Be your partner's best friend.

Respect each other – and show it by treating each other with respect.

Help without being asked.

Words your partner would like
to hear more often:

'I have faith in you.'
'I love you.'
'You did a fine job.'
'Thank you.'

❤ Appreciate what you have.

❤ Make time to be alone with each other.

❤ Cuddle early in the evening, *before* you're too tired.

If what you're doing isn't working, try something else.

Look for win/win solutions.

You can always make more money, but you can never make more time. Take time *now* for your family.

❤ When you need help, speak up!

❤ It's not enough just to say 'I love you.' *Live your love* by being considerate and kind.

❤ Leave your job – and its problems – at the office.

❤ Love has good manners.

❤ At parties, pay more attention to your partner than to anyone else.

❤ If you are having problems, figure out first the role *you* are playing.

❤ Always make your partner feel special.

❤ Give more love and you'll get more love.

❤ If you're not sure whether to say something, don't.

Kindness is love
in action

❤ Share your feelings.

❤ Call during the day, just to say 'I love you.'

❤ 50/50 isn't enough. You each have to give 100% if you want to have a *great* relationship.

❤ Turn the TV off and take time to talk together.

❤ You're part of a couple, but be your own person as well.

❤ Picture yourself as older, looking back on your life together. What do you wish you had done? *Do it now.*

❤ If you're not happy negotiate for change.

❤ Say positive affirmations about each other and your relationship.

❤ Make having fun together a priority.

Keep courting each other
after marriage

 Never go to bed mad.

 Your sweetheart needs touching and affection in *and out* of the bedroom.

 Always take each other's feelings into consideration.

❤ Kiss each other every night before turning out the lights.

❤ Plan together for the future, and then *work* to make your plans come true.

❤ Treat your partner at least as well as you treat your friends.

❤ Keep up with your individual
   hopes and dreams.

❤ Brag about each other.

❤ If your mate's always busy, make
   appointments to see each other.

❧ When your partner tells you a problem, don't rush in with a solution. Often they just want to be *heard*.

❧ Pay attention to how often you interrupt and do it less.

❤ Turn up the stereo and practise slow dancing.

❤ Be loving, even when you don't feel particularly loving.

❤ When discussions get too heated, call for a recess.

❤ Bring home flowers to your sweetheart.

❤ View the problems life gives you as challenges to be faced together.

❤ It's okay to change your mind.

❤ When you're conversing, give your undivided attention.

❤ It takes 72 muscles to frown and only 23 to smile – and smiling has *much* more pleasurable results!

Your time and attention are the most important gifts you can give

❤ Expect changes in your relationship – and work to make them positive.

❤ Visualize a bright future for the two of you.

❤ Give gifts which reflect your special knowledge of your partner.

❤️ Assure your partner often that
you care.

❤️ Let your mate know you care by
how you act.

❤️ Look for what's good in your
partner and praise it.

❤ Support each other's growth.

❤ When your partner comes home, drop what you're doing and give a big welcome at the door.

❤ Your partner will only satisfy *some* of your needs. Look to others for the rest.

Make Valentine's Day Valentine's *Week!*

If you want your mate to understand you, talk about yourself more.

Hinting hardly ever works. The best way to get what you want is to ask for it.

To encourage your mate to talk:

As you're listening, ask yourself, 'What is he feeling?' 'What is he saying?' Then answer whichever question seems more important. ('You sound upset.') Let your partner correct you or confirm that you got it right.

For Every Day's 'To Do' List:

Talk

Listen

Help out

Kiss and hug

Compliment

Express your love

❤ Honesty is important, but be tactful.

❤ Assure your partner you'll always be there.

❤ Spend more time with other couples with whom you can laugh and joke.

Write little love notes and leave them ...

On the driver's seat

In the refrigerator, taped to a favourite food

On the pillow

Inside your mate's purse or wallet

❤ Try roller skating together!

❤ Get your partner talking by asking about a hobby or sport that's of interest.

❤ One evening, hire a student who plays the violin to perform, while the two of you enjoy a candlelight dinner!

❤ Cuddle at the movies.

❤ Show you're on your partner's side.

❤ Give up trying to control the other person. The only person you can really ever control is *you*.

❤ Get up early and watch the sunrise.

❤ When criticism is true, agree with it. ('You're right. I *am* late.')

❤ Share your fantasies!

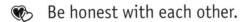 Be honest with each other.

During tough times, think of why you fell in love in the first place. Dwell on those things.

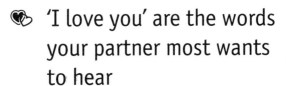 'I love you' are the words your partner most wants to hear

❤ You can disagree without being disagreeable.

❤ Treat each other in an 'I'm OK – You're OK' manner.

❤ When you feel angry, cool down before you speak up.

Express appreciation for favours.

Touch more. Touching often expresses sentiments that words alone can't convey.

Volunteer together to help a favourite charity.

Base your relationship on *your commitment to each other,* not on your feelings of love. That way, as your feelings for each other rise and fall – as they surely will – your relationship will still be secure.

❦ Instead of arguing, do problem solving.

❦ Cuddle while you watch TV.

❦ When your partner makes a mistake, don't say 'I told you so.'

❤ Surprise your mate with a spontaneous kiss.

❤ Take dance lessons together.

❤ Every once in a while, baby each other!

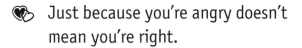 Just because you're angry doesn't mean you're right.

Ⓗ When something goes wrong, instead of assessing blame, focus on how to do better next time.

Set aside time
to be loving

❤ Play romantic games.

❤ Treat each other the way you want to be treated.

❤ It's easier in the long run to face your responsibilities.

❧ Do what makes your partner feel loved. If you don't know what that is, ask.

❧ Tell your partner when you need extra attention.

❧ Give a back rub without being asked.

❤️ Cherish each other.

❤️ Cut out articles that are likely to interest your partner.

❤️ Buy tickets, but don't say for what. The waiting and the surprise will be almost as much fun as the event.

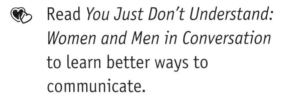 Read *You Just Don't Understand: Women and Men in Conversation* to learn better ways to communicate.

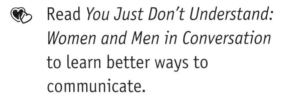 Give your mate 'Love Coupons' good for flowers, kisses, massages, etc.

Be an encourager!

What your partner needs most:

Appreciation	Understanding
Admiration	Love
Acceptance	To be cherished
Encouragement	To be cared for

❤ Make decisions when you're calm, never when you're angry.

❤ Let your mate know it's safe to tell you everything.

❤ Give lots of hugs.

❤ View your mate as a companion to enjoy life with – not a possession to ignore.

❤ When you feel short-changed, examine whether you have unrealistic expectations.

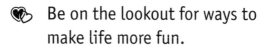 Be on the lookout for ways to make life more fun.

Write a poem. It doesn't have to be good – it just has to have your feelings in it.

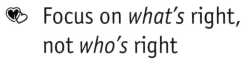 Focus on *what's* right,
not *who's* right

❤ Try out new restaurants.

❤ Rather than give good advice,
set a good example.

❤ Put a dimmer on your bedroom
light switch.

Some people express love by working hard. Let them know you understand that.

Cook your sweetheart's favourite meal.

Share what life was like when you were children.

❤ Watch '30s romances together.
Anything by Fred Astaire and
Ginger Rogers will do fine.

❤ Be grateful for your partner's love.
(Remember when you didn't
have it?)

❦ Take vacations often, even if just one night at a bed and breakfast.

❦ List all the ways your partner enriches your life. Share your list.

❦ Don't make sex the last item on your 'to do' list.

❤ To see each other's point of view,
role-play being the other person.

❤ Be tolerant. You're both fallible
human beings.

❤ Find something to like about each
other's friends.

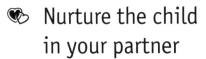 Nurture the child
in your partner

❤ Exercise together.

❤ Help your partner fulfil personal goals.

❤ View money as belonging to you both, no matter who made it.

More words your partner would like to hear more often:

'You can do it!'

'You're looking good.'

'How can I help?'

'I'm proud of you!'

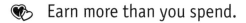 Earn more than you spend.

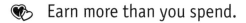 Respect the fact that your love's needs and wants may differ from yours.

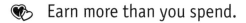 Honour each other's differences rather than trying to change them.

- Rent a rowing boat and enjoy a romantic hour on the lake.

- Save for tomorrow, but don't go completely without today.

- Be action-oriented. Instead of *waiting* for things to happen, work to *make* them happen!

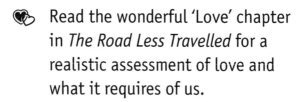

Read the wonderful 'Love' chapter in *The Road Less Travelled* for a realistic assessment of love and what it requires of us.

Go through objects each of you has saved from the past. Talk about why they're special to you.

Trust each other and be worthy of trust

❤ Judge each other with compassion, not by a standard of perfection.

❤ If both of you have jobs, it's only fair that you both share the housework. Work out a specific agreement as to who does what.

- Have a 'date night' once a week.

- Flirt more with each other.

- Consideration and kindness *out of* bed help promote good feelings *in bed*.

❤ See the opportunities inside problems.

❤ Hold hands.

❤ Mark anniversaries and birthdays on your datebook and calendar. That way you won't forget.

❤ Let your partner unwind after a long day. Bring up problems *after* dinner.

❤ Instead of confronting each other on opposite sides of the table, learn to share the same side of the table and confront your problems on the other side.

Fighting Fair – Do's

Take turns talking.

Bring up only *one* problem at a time.

Focus on the present.

Express how you feel.

Restate each others' points to their satisfaction before voicing your own opinions.

Fighting Fair – Don'ts

Interrupt

Label each other, their behaviour
or ideas

Threaten

Tell each other their motives
('You deliberately ...')

Shout, swear or hit

Write down things you have been happiest doing together in the past. Do those things more often.

Be close, but always keep some space for yourself.

 Learn to forgive

❤ Respect the privacy of each other's purse, wallet, papers and mail.

❤ Once in a while, each of you have a day which is 'yours'. On that day, you get treated extra nice and get to choose what both of you will do.

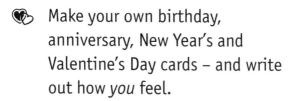 Make your own birthday, anniversary, New Year's and Valentine's Day cards – and write out how *you* feel.

Even if it's not a holiday, write a love note to your sweetheart.

- ❤ Learn to make *yourself* happy instead of relying on your partner.

- ❤ Bike ride together in the countryside.

- ❤ Learn some foreign words and phrases, so you'll have a 'secret' language the two of you can use.

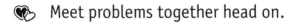 Meet problems together head on.

Look for the brightest star and make a wish.

Turn your weaknesses into strengths by filling in where each other is lacking.

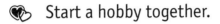 Start a hobby together.

 Realize you both want the same things: to love and be loved, to contribute and be appreciated, to have fun, and to feel secure.

❦ Asking for help doesn't mean
you're weak – just intelligent.

❦ Take a bath together, complete
with jasmine scented bath oils,
scented candles and soft music.

If you care, speak
in a caring way

❤ Overlook each other's flaws –
remembering that you have your
own.

❤ Share your dreams.

❤ Don't take each other for granted.

❤ There is no perfect love out there waiting for you. *Enjoy the one you have.*

❤ When you hurt your partner, say you're sorry.

❤ Dress up for each other.

Criticize only in private.

When you present a gift, wrap it beautifully. Your effort will be appreciated.

You may not always agree, but always hear each other out.

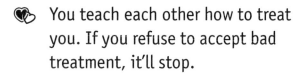 You teach each other how to treat you. If you refuse to accept bad treatment, it'll stop.

Never assume marriage will change either of you.

❤ You can make mistakes and still be okay.

❤ Avoid comparing yourselves with other couples. You'll never know the truth about them, and it's wiser to just enjoy your own happiness.

❤ Humour is healing – and it's fun too!

❤ Get a guidebook for your area, and explore the places you haven't yet visited.

❤ Put each other before all others, including your parents and friends.

❤ When things go wrong, accept your part of the responsibility.

❤ Show you're open to conversation by keeping your legs and arms uncrossed.

❤ Buy gifts that say, 'I love you' – no pots and pans.

To be interesting,
be interested

 Admire each other's achievements.

Thank your partner for compliments and kind gestures – and you'll get more of them!

❧ Not *all* your mate's problems are *your* problems. Sometimes it's better to be uninvolved.

❧ Have your partner be your best friend – not your only friend.

❧ Play tennis or ping-pong together.

❤ Nurture and protect the things you love about your partner.

❤ Ask yourself how you can add to your relationship, instead of what more you can get from it.

❦ Never bring up past loves.

❦ 'Peace at any Price' leads to temporary peace at a high price. Better to work things out.

❦ Spend your energy fixing problems rather than assigning blame.

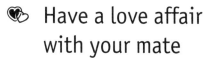 Have a love affair
with your mate

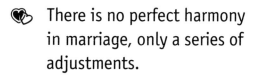 There is no perfect harmony
in marriage, only a series of
adjustments.

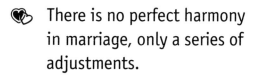 Use things, not people. Love
people, not things.

💕 Recognize each other's contributions to the family.

💕 Surprise your partner with breakfast in bed.

💕 Give your love unconditionally.

Take time for yourself too

- Happy marriages come from balanced exchanges.

- If you feel resentful, start asking for what you want more.

- If you feel guilty, start giving more.

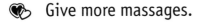 Give more massages.

Go on lots of walks together, arm-in-arm.

Thank your partner for doing household chores.

Keep your promises

❤ Be faithful.

❤ Go to bed early and talk in the dark.

❤ Buy frivolous things for your partner that she wouldn't buy for herself.

❤ Propose a toast to your mate,
even though you've only got water
in your glass!

❤ Write each other a note saying
how the other person has changed
your life for the better.

❤❤ When you're angry, *think* before you speak.

❤❤ View things that go wrong as 'unfortunate' – not horrible. Most of what we 'awfulize' about, we won't even remember in a few days.

Focus on the 90% that's right – not the 10% that isn't

💕 Have a professional photo taken of the two of you.

💕 Your relationship is like a bank account: you have to put into it before you can take out of it.

❤️ Cuddle often, even when you don't want sex.

❤️ Take in more live theatre.

❤️ The time you spend counts far more than the money you spend.

💕 Keep a scrapbook of your favourite moments together. Look through it on rainy days.

💕 If expressing your feelings is hard for you, write them out.

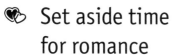 Set aside time
for romance

❤ Let your partner know you find her attractive.

❤ It's okay to disagree.

❤ When your mate comes home from a trip, put up a poster saying, 'WELCOME HOME!'

- Reaffirm your vows in front of your friends and family.

- Develop common goals.

- Take the phone off the hook during intimate moments.

Ask more open-ended questions.

They begin with 'how', 'why', and 'tell me about' – and they encourage your partner to open up.
(*'Tell me about the highlight of your day.' 'Why are you so eager to see the exhibit?'*)

Don't ask too open-ended questions.

They ask for *so* much information, all you get are one or two word answers.
(*'Tell me all about your day.'*
'What's new at work?')

 Be outrageous once in a while.

 The best way to encourage your partner to change is to change yourself.

❤ Your first task is to manage your own life.

❤ Flatter your partner.

❤ When your mate's almost done bathing, sneak the towel out of the bathroom – and warm it in the dryer!

Have priorities
and make love first –
not last

❤ Your feelings come from your thinking. If you change your thoughts about your mate, your feelings will change.

❤ Instead of criticizing what you don't like, praise what you do like.

❤ Tackle problems early, while they're small, while there are still lots of good feelings.

❤ Write out together 10 things you'd love to do together. Then, get started doing them!

Always take care
of each other

By the same author:

THE PARENTS' LITTLE
INSTRUCTION BOOK

... Coming Soon!

A Baby's Little
Instruction Book

- Learn which parent is the softest touch
- Pester to be taken out to play when Mummy's got a hangover
- Talk with your mouth full
- Remember that 'Don't touch' is a licence to handle things
- Scream in the supermarket
- Learn to open child safety locks
- Don't speak if pointing will do

Life's Little Instruction Book
Volume II

- Talk slowly but think quickly
- Never claim a victory prematurely
- Don't open credit card bills at the weekend
- Never be the first to break a family tradition
- Put your address inside your luggage as well as on the outside
- Take off the conference badge as soon as you leave the venue
- Check the toilet paper *before* sitting down